MYSTERIES OF THE UNEXPLAINED

Written by Sue Crawford, Rupert Matthews,
Ben Wilson and John Wright

Illustrated by Gordon C Davies, Peter Dennis, Tony Gibbons,
Martin Kingstone, Bernard Long and Nik Spender

WORLD INTERNATIONAL PUBLISHING LIMITED
MANCHESTER

Copyright © 1988, 1989 Wayland (Publishers) Limited.
This edition published in Great Britain in 1991 by
World International Publishing Limited in association with
Wayland (Publishers) Limited. All rights reserved.
World International Publishing Limited, an Egmont Company,
Egmont House, PO Box 111, Great Ducie Street, Manchester M60 3BL.
Printed in Singapore.
ISBN 0 7498 0440 8

Author and Illustrator Credits
Written by Sue Crawford (pages 6–11), Rupert Matthews (pages 12–17, 36–55),
Ben Wilson (pages 18–23, 30–35, 56–61) and John Wright (pages 24–29).
Illustrated by Marilyn Clay (pages 9, 26, 28); Gordon C Davies (pages 56–60);
Peter Dennis (pages 6–8, 10–11, 42–47); Tony Gibbons (pages 18, 19, 22,
23, 30–32, 35); Martin Kingstone (pages 20, 33); Bernard Long (pages 24,
25, 27, 36–41, 48–50, 53–55); Nik Spender (pages 12–17); Stephen Wheele
(pages 39, 51, 52, 61).

Picture Acknowledgements
Wayland (Publishers) Limited would like to thank the following for supplying pictures for use in this
book: BBC Hulton Picture Library p10 upper; Fortrean Picture Library p21, p55 top (Nicholas
Witchell), p55 bottom, p61 top; The Hutchinson Library p15; Mary Evans Picture Library p8 lower,
p9; Mountain Camera p39 (top), p41 left and right (John Cleare); Photri p28, p54, p59; Sheridan
Photo Library p8 upper; South American Pictures p10 lower; Topham p16 bottom, p38, p46, p51
bottom; Zefa p14, p16 top.

No part of this publication may be reproduced, stored in a retrieval system, or
transmitted, in any form or by any means, electronic, mechanical, photocopying,
recording or otherwise, without the prior permission of the publishers.

Contents

Atlantis — at last?   6
    Plato's paradise

A Celtic ceremony   12
    The standing stones

The Flying Dutchman — fact or fiction?   18
    Ghosts and ghost ships

Digging for the Oak Island treasure   24
    The 'money pit'

Vanished without trace!   30
    The ships' graveyard

King Arthur's body found?   36
    The search for Camelot

Did author foretell sinking of the Titanic?   42
    Glimpsing the future

A sea monster's deathly grip   48
    Monsters of the deep

The Mantell mystery   56
    Out of this world?

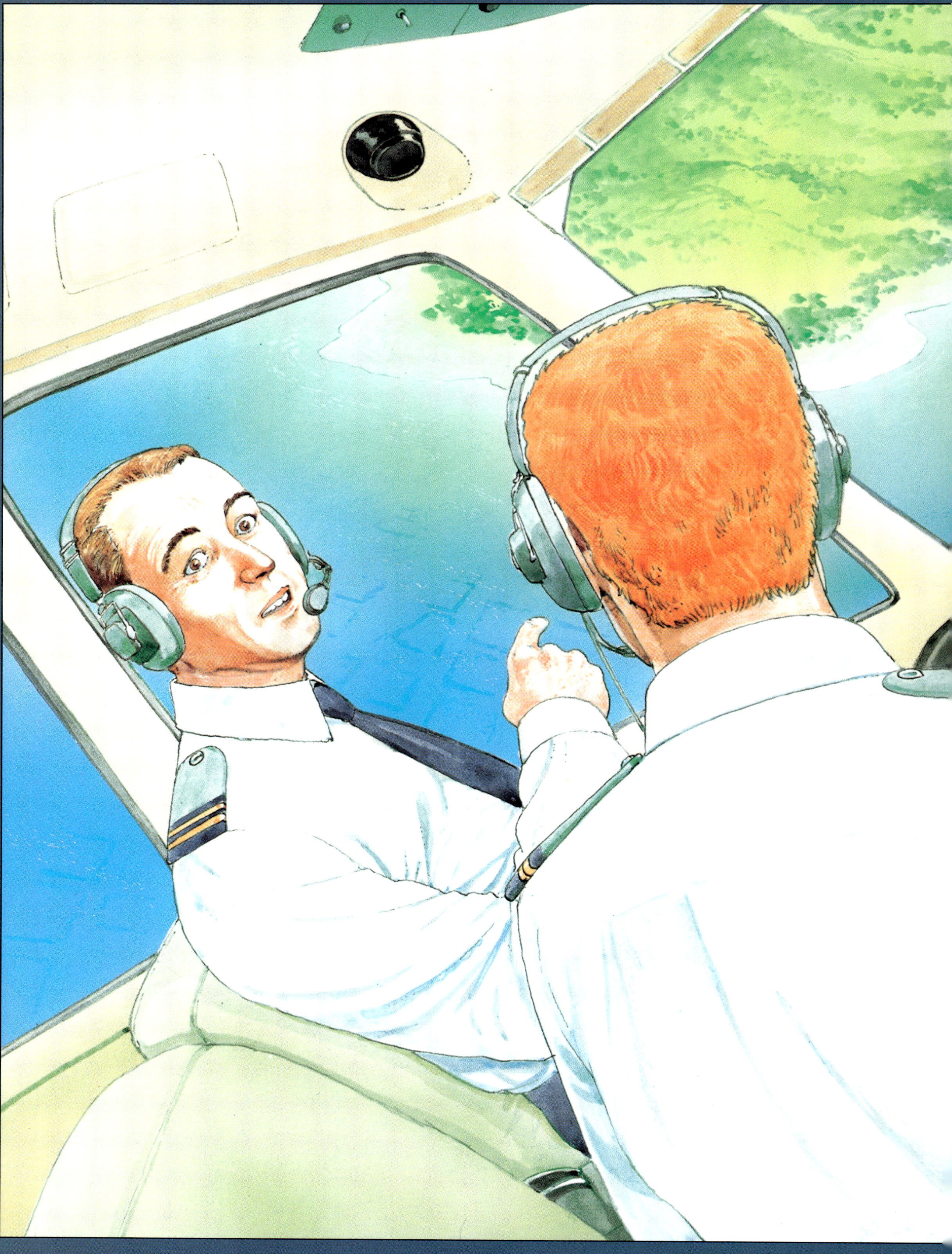

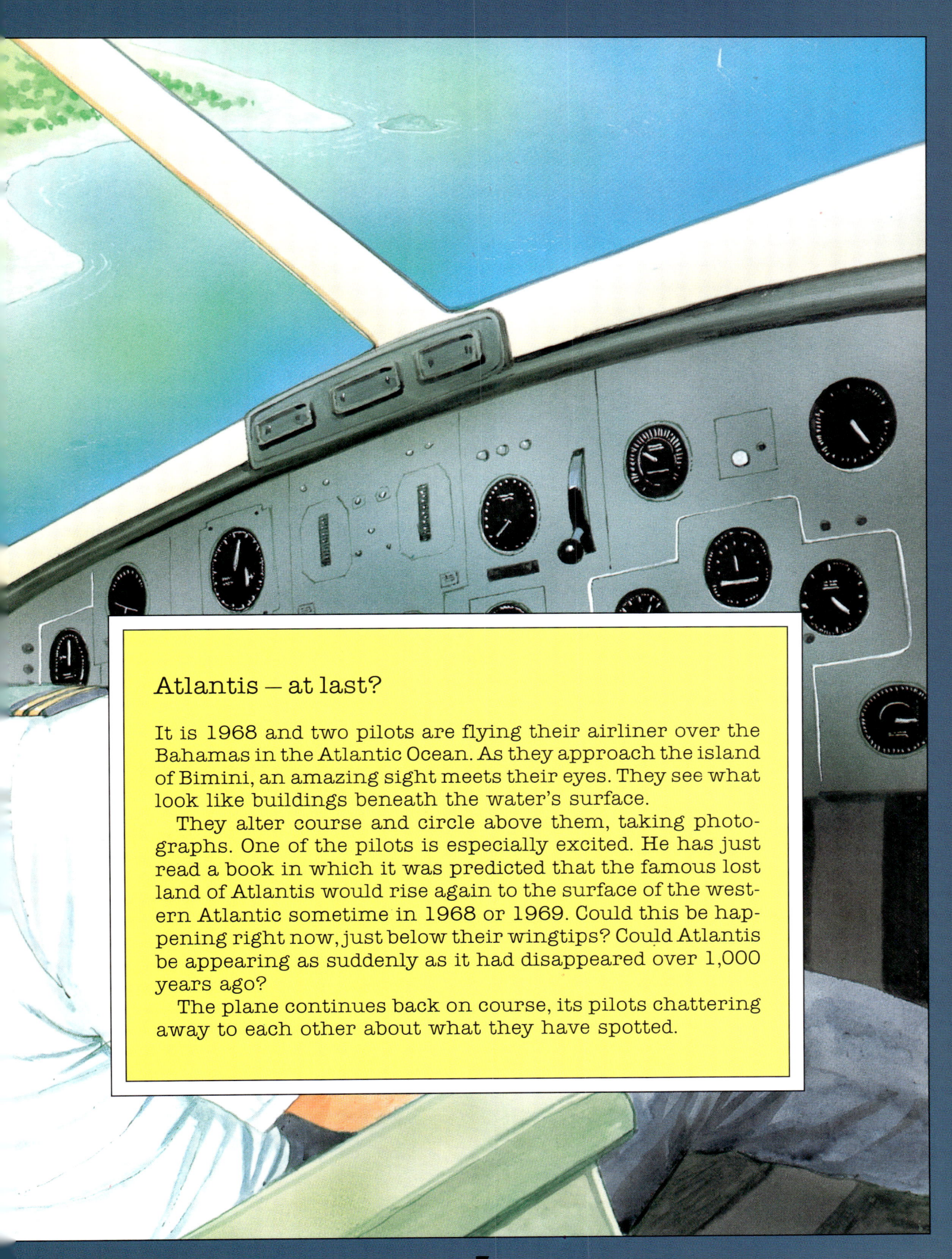

Atlantis — at last?

It is 1968 and two pilots are flying their airliner over the Bahamas in the Atlantic Ocean. As they approach the island of Bimini, an amazing sight meets their eyes. They see what look like buildings beneath the water's surface.

They alter course and circle above them, taking photographs. One of the pilots is especially excited. He has just read a book in which it was predicted that the famous lost land of Atlantis would rise again to the surface of the western Atlantic sometime in 1968 or 1969. Could this be happening right now, just below their wingtips? Could Atlantis be appearing as suddenly as it had disappeared over 1,000 years ago?

The plane continues back on course, its pilots chattering away to each other about what they have spotted.

Plato's paradise

Atlantis is the most famous of the lost lands. The Greek philosopher Plato was the first person to write about this massive continent which, he said, lay in the middle of the Atlantic Ocean nearly 12,000 years ago. He described it as a paradise, where the people were wise, highly skilled and just; the cities carefully organized and well built; and the countryside beautiful.

Then, in the space of a single day and a night, disaster struck. A terrific storm hit Atlantis, bringing with it hurricane-force winds and tidal waves. Atlantis and her people sank beneath the ocean's waves, leaving no trace of their existence.

This story has given ideas to many writers, poets, film-makers and painters, but is there any truth in it? Or is Atlantis just everyone's dream of an ideal world, free from all evil?

Plato claimed that his descriptions of Atlantis were based on ancient Egyptian writings, but these have never been found – all we do know is that the Egyptian who translated them for Plato did exist. Since then, many explorers have searched the world for remains of Atlantis, saying they have discovered it in the Atlantic, in the Mediterranean Sea, and even in the Pacific.

A carving of Plato, the famous Greek philosopher. He was the first person to mention the lost continent of Atlantis.

According to Sir Gerald Hargreaves, writing in the 1950s, one of the main squares of Atlantis would have looked like this.

Some people think that the continent of Atlantis did not disappear overnight, but gradually broke up. They say it split into two main areas: (1) Antillia and (2) Atlantis. While the latter has vanished completely, bits of Antillia still remain – the Antilles, a group of islands in the Caribbean.

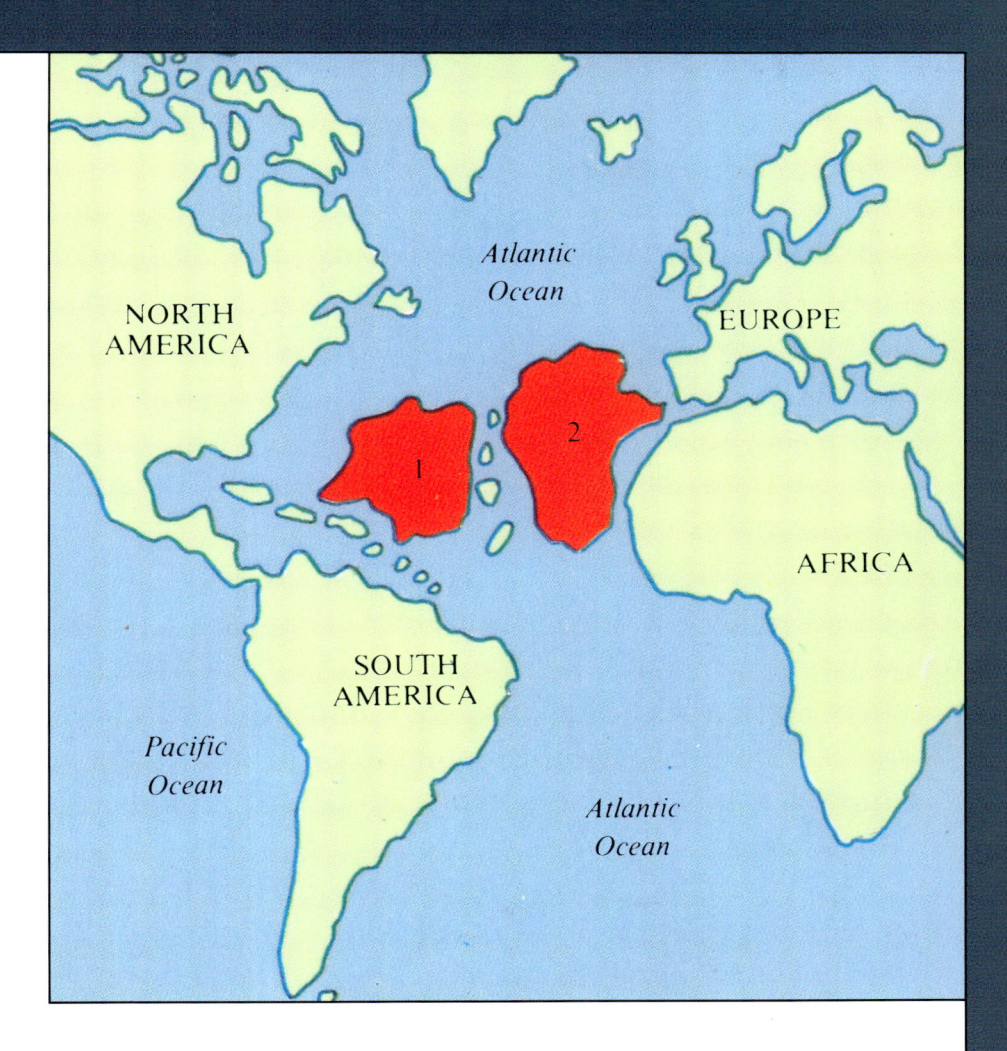

The presence of thick seaweed, which is often a sign of shallow water, in the Sargasso Sea area of the Atlantic, has been used by some people to show that Atlantis may be slowly coming to the surface there. Francis Bacon, the seventeenth-century British philosopher, thought that North America was Atlantis.

Another view of Sir Gerald Hargreaves's Atlantis. Do you think Atlantis would have looked like this?

A detailed book

In 1882, an American author, Ignatius Donnelly, published his book *Atlantis: the Antediluvian World*. It has become one of the most important works on the subject. In it, Donnelly provided a very detailed description of every aspect of Atlantis and said this land was the source of everything in the world today. The book is still read and appreciated for its high level of learning. However, many of its facts have been shown to be wrong or highly unlikely.

Olof Rudbeck, writing at the same time, argued that it was his homeland, Sweden. In the 1800s, a British Army officer in India suggested that the British Isles were the remains of the lost land. None of these people, however, has been able to provide any proof to back up their claims.

In the 1930s, an American medium, Edgar Cayce, predicted that the western section of Atlantis would reappear near the Bahamas in 1968 or 1969. Strangely enough, in 1968, several underwater rock formations, including what appeared to be ruined buildings and a road, were sighted off Bimini in the Bahamas. Divers went down and discovered the road to be 1 km long and made out of large, square stone blocks. One explanation of this road is that it is a natural rock formation. People who oppose this argument say that the square blocks differ from the rocks found underneath them.

There have been many other sightings in this area of the Atlantic. Everything from underwater pyramids, like those in Egypt, to circles of high stones, similar to Stonehenge in Britain, has been reported. A long flight of steps has been seen off the coast of Puerto Rico. It has also been claimed that the Russians have found a group of buildings, covering 4 hectares, off the northern coast of Cuba.

Even if all these are the remains of Atlantis, how did it disappear so quickly? Plato wrote that Atlantis was destroyed almost overnight by a storm of enormous force. However, scientists argue that it takes millions of years for a large area of land to sink beneath the waves or to rise again. They say that it is impossible for

Above *Ignatius Donnelly, who wrote one of the most important books on the subject of Atlantis.* **Below** *Edgar Cayce, who said that the western section of Atlantis would reappear near the Bahamas in 1968 or 1969.*

Divers investigating the underwater 'road' off the island of Bimini, in the Bahamas.

Atlantis to have sunk so quickly or to have started to reappear now. Nevertheless, supporters of the Atlantis theory reply that certain natural events, like an enormous meteor landing from outer space or a volcanic eruption, have in the past caused such large-scale disasters that stories about them appear in the writings of every people in the world. Perhaps the destruction of Atlantis was one of these natural occurrences, and stories about it have been handed down from generation to generation?

Airships in Atlantis?

According to W. Scott-Elliot, the people of Atlantis were so advanced that they had built airships. They were powered by a mysterious fuel which we have yet to discover! They could travel at speeds of 140 kph and were made out of a metal which shone in the dark, as if coated with luminous paint! As well as passenger airships, military ones were built which could hold between 50 and 100 men!

A Celtic ceremony

It is dark. The eastern sky has begun to lighten, but no rays of sunshine light the scene. A large group of people dressed in long, white robes approach the stones. They walk along the pathway between two earthen banks which run up the hill from the northeast. Three men lead the group.

　　The procession reaches the circular bank and passes silently within the sacred enclosure. The three leaders pass between two stones and enter the great circle of upright stones. Most of the people remain outside the stone circle. They strain to see what the three men are doing.

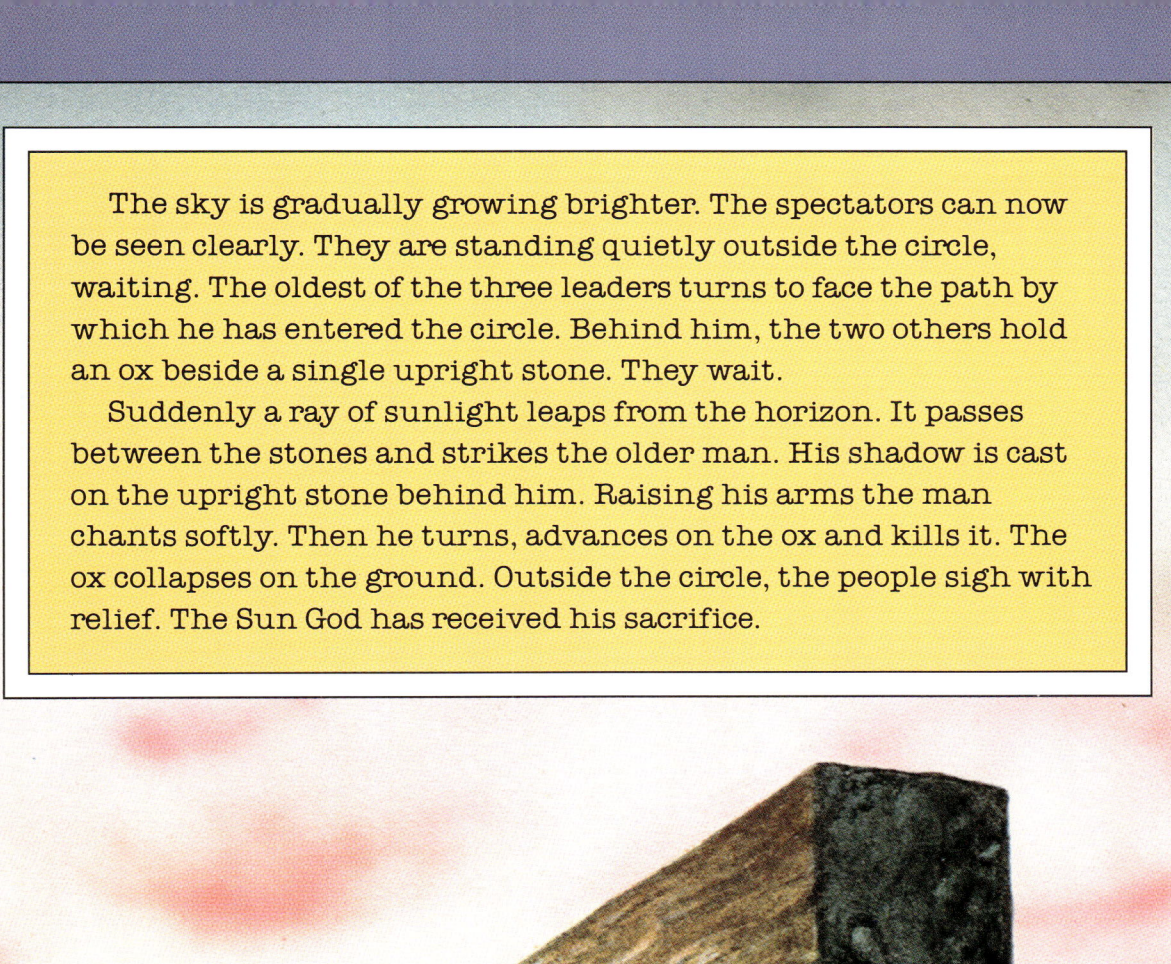

The sky is gradually growing brighter. The spectators can now be seen clearly. They are standing quietly outside the circle, waiting. The oldest of the three leaders turns to face the path by which he has entered the circle. Behind him, the two others hold an ox beside a single upright stone. They wait.

Suddenly a ray of sunlight leaps from the horizon. It passes between the stones and strikes the older man. His shadow is cast on the upright stone behind him. Raising his arms the man chants softly. Then he turns, advances on the ox and kills it. The ox collapses on the ground. Outside the circle, the people sigh with relief. The Sun God has received his sacrifice.

The standing stones

The gaunt outline of Stonehenge rises above the slopes of Salisbury Plain in southern England. The vast circle of standing stones lies beside a main road and is easy both to find and to visit.

The ruined stone monument is impressive by its size. The tallest stones are 6.7 metres high and weigh around fifty tonnes. However, the way in which these huge stones are assembled seems little short of amazing.

Archaeologists and historians have been interested in Stonehenge for many years. During the eighteenth century, it was believed that Stonehenge had been built by the druids. These priests were Celts who came to Britain from France and Germany about 450 BC. The druids offered humans in bloody ceremonies of sacrifice. It was therefore thought that Stonehenge might have been a temple in which sacrifice was common.

At dawn, the circle of Stonehenge is silhouetted against the rising sun.

During the twentieth century, fresh excavations at Stonehenge have yielded much important information. The first construction on the site, now occupied by Stonehenge, was the bank and ditch which can still be seen. This circular earthwork is the 'henge' of Stonehenge, constructed about 3200BC. It is thought that within the ditch was built a large, circular wooden building. This may have been used to keep dead bodies. Such buildings are known as charnel houses.

Also erected at this early time was the Heel Stone, which stands outside the circular bank. It is clear that this monument was constructed so that it aligned with the moon. The entrance to the henge faced the most northerly moonrise, which only occurs once in eighteen years. The Heel Stone, meanwhile, marked the place on the horizon where the moon would be seen to rise part way through this eighteen year cycle.

The central circle of Stonehenge is seen here through the main entrance of the henge: a circular bank and ditch that surrounds the stone monument.

Right *The largest sarsen stones at Stonehenge form the central trilithons — a group of three stones, as shown here.*

Below *In 1958 government scientists excavated Stonehenge and re-erected some of the fallen stones.*

It seems that after many years of use, the henge and its wooden building were abandoned. It was not until about 2200BC that new building work was carried out.

About eighty boulders of bluestone were brought to the site and erected in a double circle at the centre of the henge. The origin of these bluestones is a mystery in itself. The nearest source for this particular type of stone is in the Prescelly Mountains of South Wales, 210 kilometres from Stonehenge.

The new Stonehenge was very different from the old structure. Not only was stone used, instead of timber, but it faced the midsummer sunrise. It is thought that a new people may have brought a new religion to the area.

Around Stonehenge

Stonehenge lies at the centre of a vast area of prehistoric sites. One of the most mysterious is the Great Cursus, as nobody knows why it is there or what purpose it once served. It is made up of two earth banks about one metre high and one hundred metres apart which run for three kilometres across Salisbury Plain.

Before the bluestone circles were completed they were demolished. New, larger stones, known as sarsens, were brought to the site from the Marlborough Downs, about 32 kilometres to the north.

Once at Stonehenge, the sarsens were shaped and placed upright in pits dug to hold them. The horizontal stones, known as lintels, were then raised and placed on top of these upright sarsens.

The most obvious explanation for this monument is that it was a temple of some kind. However, it has been found that the many stones are relevant to dozens of different astronomical events. It has therefore been suggested that Stonehenge was a type of astronomical observatory.

Whatever the true purpose of Stonehenge, be it charnel house, observatory, temple or sacrificial altar, it remains one of the most mysterious structures in Britain. For thousands of years, the stones have stood on their windswept site on Salisbury Plain. Let us hope that they remain there for many years to come, until one day their mystery is revealed.

Date Chart

3200BC Stonehenge I, a timber building surrounded by a bank and ditch is erected. After several centuries it is abandoned.

2200BC About eighty bluestones are brought from Wales and erected to form Stonehenge II.

2000BC Stonehenge II is demolished. Sarsen stones are brought to the site and Stonehenge III is erected.

1500BC The bluestones are returned to Stonehenge and erected within the sarsen circle.

About **1000BC** Stonehenge is abandoned.

Stonehenge is one of the most famous stone monuments in northwest Europe. This structure, also used as a burial chamber, is Kits Coty House in Kent.

The Flying Dutchman — fact or fiction?

In the early seventeenth century, Captain Hendrik van der Decken sets sail from Amsterdam aboard the *Flying Dutchman*. He is bound for the East Indies. A greedy and foolish man, he is determined to make his fortune on this trip.

All goes well until the ship begins to round the dangerous waters of the Cape of Good Hope. For days fierce storms batter the ship. In spite of the pleas of the passengers and the crew to seek sheltered waters, Captain van der Decken heartlessly pursues his course. He drinks and smokes, pausing only to fill the air with curses.

Suddenly, a strange form appears on deck. It announces that it is the Devil and challenges van der Decken to oppose God's will by sailing into the teeth of the storm. The Dutch captain agrees . . . and brings down God's curse on his head:

> 'You are condemned to sail on until the Day of Judgement, without rest and without ever making land.'

From that day onwards, the *Flying Dutchman* is doomed to roam the seas, bringing ill fortune and disaster on any vessel which might cross her path. The tale of the ghost ship might seem to be the stuff of legend. But there are numerous accounts of those people who claim to have seen her . . . and suffered as a result!

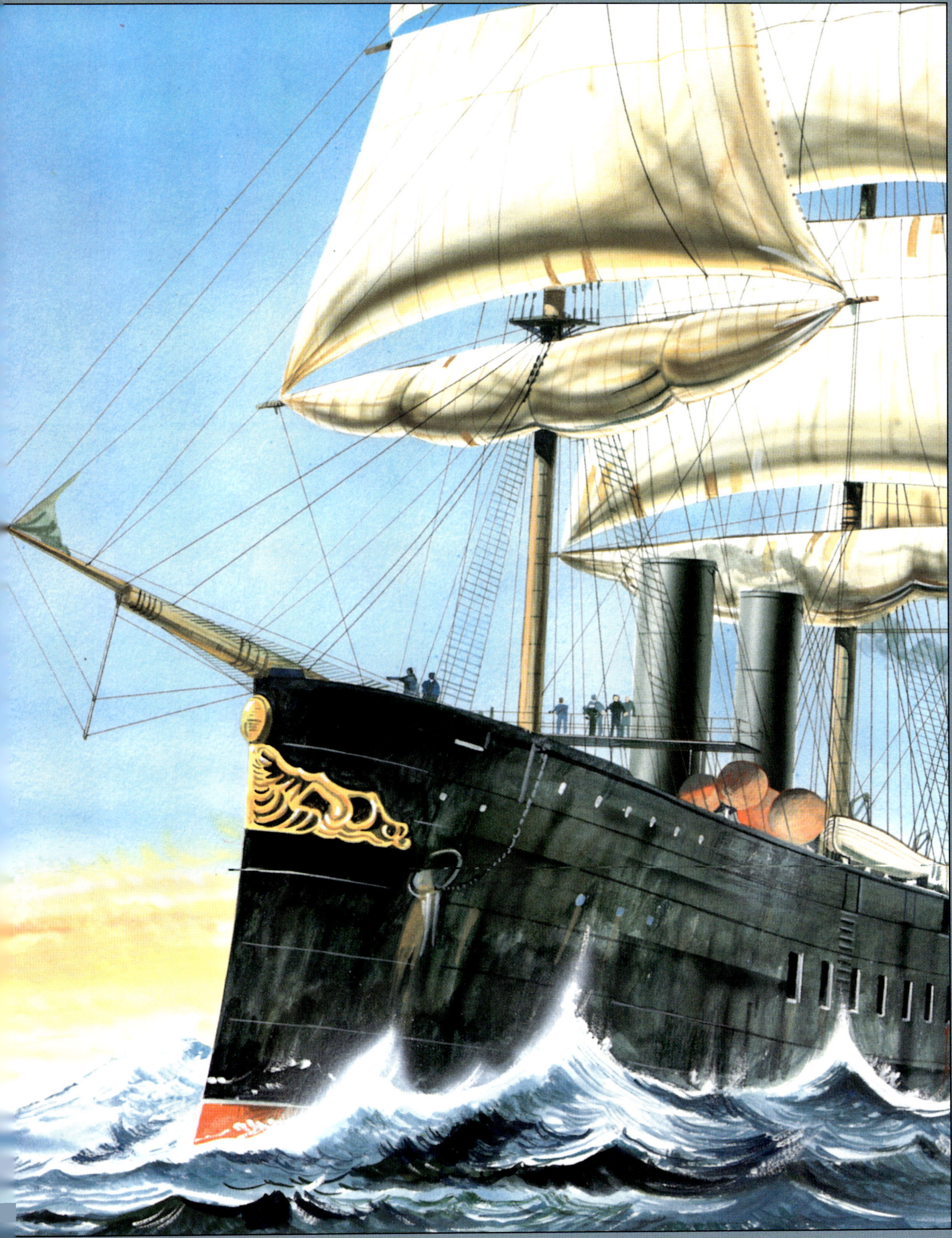

Ghosts and ghost ships

The sea has been a place of danger and death for many sailors. As a result, a number of superstitions and legends have arisen about those lost at sea and the ships they sailed in. Most of these, of course, are the work of many a sailor's vivid imagination told and re-told with ever more fantastic details added. But there remains a handful of genuinely puzzling ghostly sea mysteries which still send a tingle of fear down the spine.

Mystery surrounds the tale of the *Ourang Medan*, a Dutch freighter which was bound for Jakarta, Indonesia, in February 1948. On a day of calm seas and clear blue skies, she sent out the following SOS call which was picked up by over a dozen ships:

'Captain and all officers dead. Entire crew dead or dying. Now I am also near death'.

A grim sight awaited the rescue team which reached the stricken vessel three hours later. The deck was littered with

Was it a horrific monster that terrified the crew of the Ourang Medan *to death in 1948? We will never know.*

corpses, while on the bridge lay the dead bodies of the officers and the captain. Each man appeared to have died in the same way, eyes fixed in horror and arms raised to the sky. Even the ship's dog lay with its fangs bared and its paws arched in the air, as if trying to ward off an invisible enemy. The rescue team's doctor could find no trace of poisoning, disease or of any fumes that might have caused the deaths. What was the cause? The question has never been answered satisfactorily.

Why should a photograph of two men swimming in the Pacific be one of the most remarkable ever taken? Because the two men, James Courtenay and Michael Meehan, had been killed four days before the photograph was taken! They had been overcome by poisonous fumes while working in the engine room of the oil tanker, *Waterton*. On 3 December 1929, the day after they had been buried at sea, an astonished deckhand spotted the two men swimming just 15 metres from the tanker. Over the course of the next three days, the men were to appear frequently, smiling and waving at their astonished crewmates. On the tanker's next voyage, a member of the crew managed to take eight photographs of Courtenay and Meehan. Unfortunately, only one of the photos gave a clear picture. But, it was enough. Friends and relatives of the two men had no doubt that the two swimmers were Courtenay and Meehan!

Perhaps the most well-known sea mystery is that of the *Marie Celeste*, the 'ghost ship' found adrift off the Azores on 3 December 1872. There was no sign of life on board, either above or below decks. There were no clues to explain why the crew had disappeared. Indeed everything appeared to be quite normal. In the crew's quarters, clothing lay folded neatly on bunks and washing hung on lines. In the galley,

One of the photographs taken of Courtenay and Meehan, swimming next to the tanker Waterton, *after they had been killed by poisonous fumes in the ship's engine room.*

The ghost ship of the Goodwins

The *Lady Lovibond* ran aground on the Goodwin Sands, off south-east England, on 13 February 1748. At the time a wedding celebration was being held on board. Fifty years later to the day, a three-masted schooner identical to the *Lady Lovibond* was seen heading towards the Goodwins. Voices and laughing could be heard, followed by screams of terror as she ran aground. On both 13 February 1848 and 1898, the same ghostly sight was seen, and the same sounds of joy followed by horror. In 1948, many people watched for her, but nothing was seen. Will she return in 1998?

breakfast had been prepared and some of it had been served. In the captain's cabin, breakfast had been left. Next to it, the captain's log showed entries up to 25 November and gave no hint of anything being wrong.

Why was the *Marie Celeste* abandoned? It seems unlikely that bad weather was the cause. There was little sign of damage on deck and the ship had taken in only a normal amount of water. Was there a mutiny? There was no sign of a struggle and, in any case, why would the mutineers have left the ship too?

Instead of answers, there remains one final question. How did the *Marie Celeste* remain on her intended course for ten days and some 800 km with no one at the wheel to steer her? Stories grew up that the ship was cursed. Although she was recovered and put to sea again, she had an unhappy history. She was sold 17 times in 11 years before being run aground deliberately off the coast of Haiti in 1884, taking her terrible secret to a watery grave.

What made the captain of the Marie Celeste *abandon his ship, along with his crew, half-way through his breakfast?*

The ghost of the UB65

The Second Officer of the German UB65 submarine was killed when one of her own torpedoes accidently exploded in her hold. For months after the accident, the Second Officer was seen by members of the crew in different parts of the submarine. One crewman was driven mad by the ghost's presence and threw himself overboard to his doom. Even a pastor could not rid the submarine of her unwanted visitor. Finally, on 10 July 1918, just as the UB65 was about to be attacked by an American submarine, the German vessel was ripped apart by a terrible explosion from within. Could the ghost of the UB65 have taken its terrible and final revenge?

Digging for the Oak Island treasure

It is a sunny summer's day in 1795. Sixteen-year-old Daniel McGinnis has paddled his canoe across Mahone Bay in Nova Scotia, on Canada's Atlantic coast, to the island known locally as Oak Island. After beaching the canoe in a sandy inlet, he goes exploring. Soon he finds himself in a clearing, in the centre of which stands an old oak tree. A weather-beaten block and tackle dangles from one of its branches, which has been cut short. Beneath it, Daniel notices that the ground has sunk into a saucer-like depression. Someone had once dug a hole there. Could this be the place where pirates had buried the treasure that is often mentioned by local people?

Back home, Daniel tells his two friends, Anthony Vaughan, aged 13, and John Smith, 20, about his discovery. The next day, equipped with rope, picks and shovels, all three return to Oak Island. When they have dug a wide hole, just over a metre deep, Daniel's shovel strikes a solid object – a layer of flagstones. Excitedly, the boys raise them, only to see loose earth underneath. But they are not disappointed, because finding the flagstones convinces them that something really does lie in the ground below them, so they continue digging. At a depth of 3 metres, they come across a layer of oak logs, and another layer 3 metres further down. Realizing that it is too dangerous to go on, the boys decide to get help.

The 'money pit'

After discovering the flagstones and the layers of logs, Daniel and his friends returned to their homes, in the town of Chester, and told their parents what they had been doing all day. They did not share their sons' enthusiasm for the hidden treasure and did all they possibly could to discourage them from returning to the island, even warning them that it was still haunted. Not until 1804, nine years later, did the boys find a group of people who would provide the money for the equipment they needed to dig deeper.

By then, the walls of the hole had collapsed, but Daniel and his team soon cleared it out and resumed the digging. Three metres below the second layer of oak logs, another layer was found, and so it continued, with logs being unearthed every 3 metres to a depth of 27 metres. The gaps between some of the logs were sealed with coconut fibre and ship's putty. At this point, a large stone was revealed, with

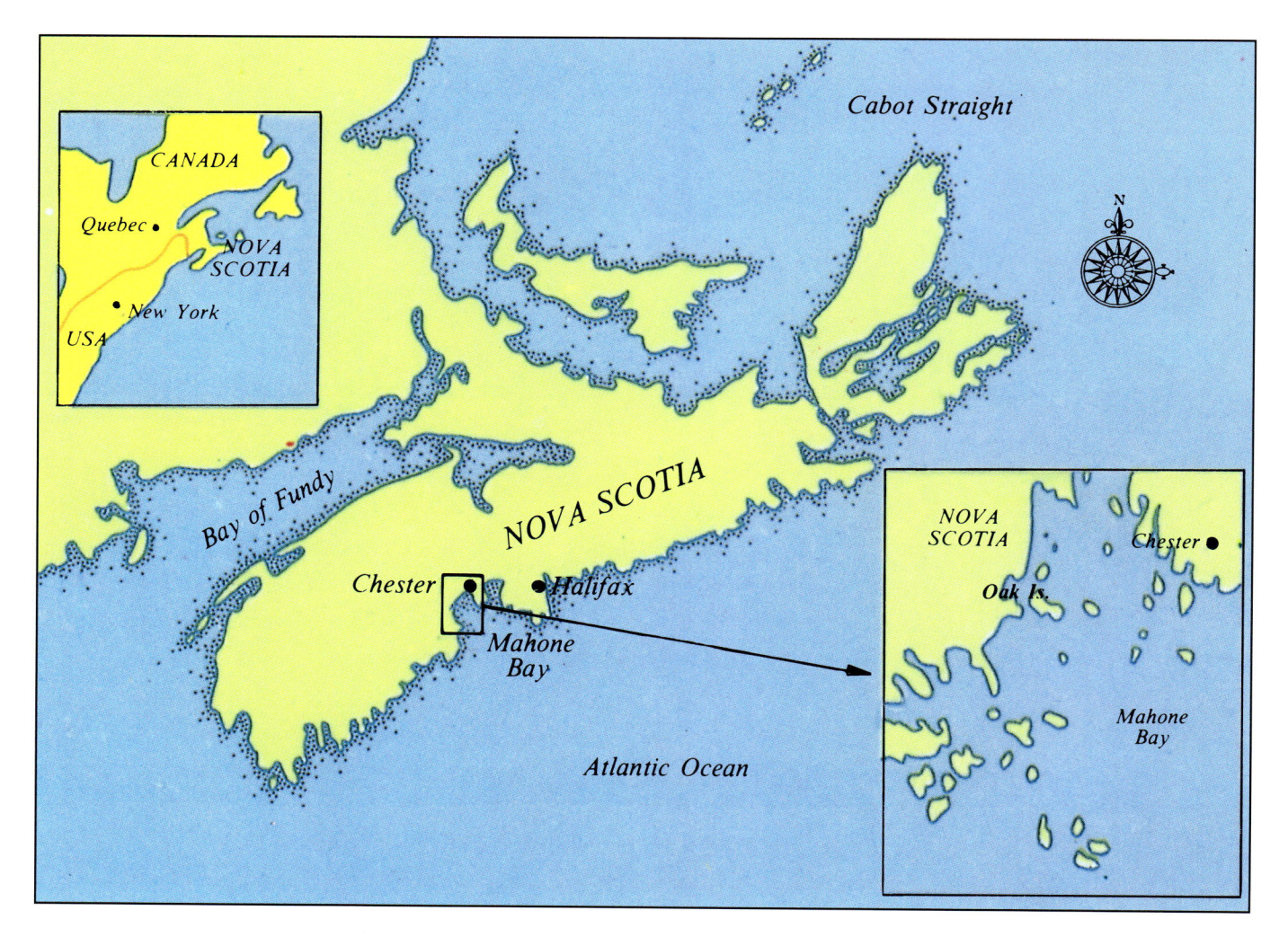

Ghosts

Oak Island is supposed to be haunted by the ghosts of pirates who used to visit it. In the past, strange lights and fires have been seen there and a party of local people vanished when they rowed out to investigate them.

Above *Daniel and his team at work on Oak Island (see the map **opposite**) in 1804.*

the words 'ten feet below, two million pounds' in code on it. The diggers were convinced that they had almost reached their goal. They stopped, reluctantly, for the night. The next morning everyone was horrified to find their shaft flooded with water, almost to the top. Full of gloom, they began to pump it out. But despite all their efforts, the water remained at the same level. They tried again the following day, but it was no use and the project had to be abandoned.

Another attempt was made in the spring of 1805. The shaft, now called the 'Money Pit', had caved in yet again, so the team decided to sink another one alongside it and then tunnel through to the old one. Just after they had broken through into the original shaft, the new one began to fill up with water. Once more, they admitted defeat and gave up.

Forty years later, in 1849, another group of people, called the Truro Syndicate, tried to reach the treasure. Anthony Vaughan was the only member from the previous teams to be involved. The Money Pit was dug out again until flooding stopped all work. This time it was decided to drill five narrow holes, 32 metres deep, to find out what was

The cost

To find the treasure on Oak Island: over $3,000,000 has been spent; over 20 shafts have been dug, and 6 men have lost their lives.

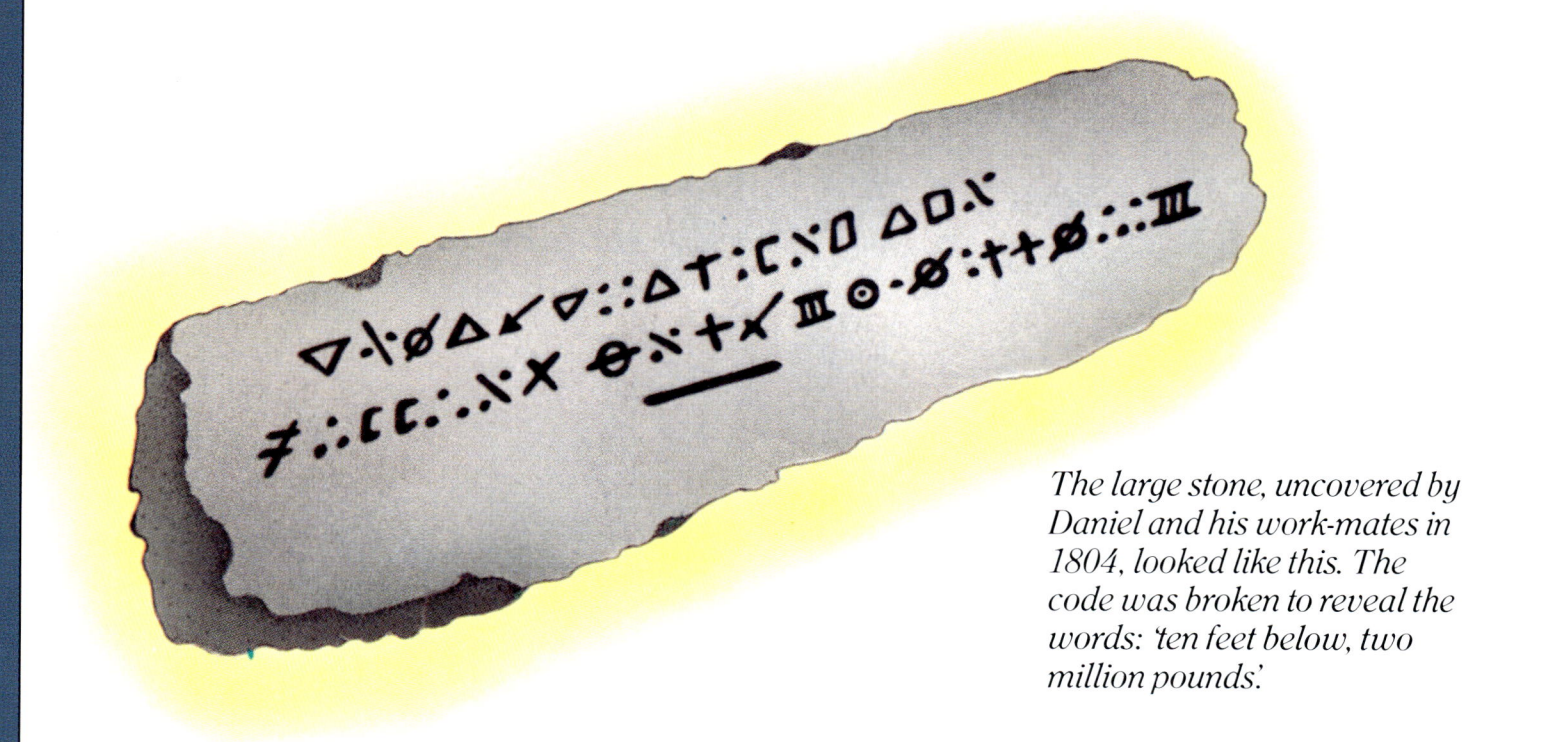

The large stone, uncovered by Daniel and his work-mates in 1804, looked like this. The code was broken to reveal the words: 'ten feet below, two million pounds'.

below the shaft. Samples brought up by the drills revealed that there were two oak chests down there, one above the other on a layer of logs. Encouraged by this news, which seemed to confirm that the Money Pit had been built to hide something valuable, a third shaft was dug to the west of the original one. It, too, became flooded. Where did all the water come from? By accident, a man fell into the shaft and swallowed what tasted like salty sea-water. After a careful search around the shore of Oak Island, the syndicate discovered the entrance to an underground tunnel. It looked as though sea-water, trapped in the tunnel, would flood the Money Pit if people broke the air-tight 'seal' made by the layers of logs. Whoever had dug the Money Pit had been a very clever engineer. How could the syndicate stop the sea-water entering the tunnel?

Builders began constructing a dam to prevent the water getting into the tunnel. But the sea washed it away before it was finished. In desperation, dynamite was used to blow up the tunnel. Even so, water continued to flood the Money Pit. Disaster followed on disaster until the Truro Syndicate's money ran out. Once more, all work on the Money Pit had to cease.

Since 1849, many attempts have been made to find the treasure. In 1972, a team of treasure seekers sank a shaft to over 45 metres. It, too, filled with water. Perhaps there was a

The town of Chester, on Mahone Bay, where Daniel McGinnis and his friends lived.

THE MONEY PIT

Oak tree with sawn-off branch
Block and tackle
Layer of flagstones
Oak platforms (every 3 metres) — 3 metres
6
9
— — — — — — — — — — — — Tide level
With putty seal — 12
15
With putty and coconut fibre seal — 18
21
24
Stone with message — 27
Treasure chests — 30
Tunnel to the sea
Clay and mud
Second tunnel
Treasure chamber?

A cross-section of the main shaft of the Money Pit on Oak Island. Will we ever know what lies at its base?

second tunnel beneath the first one? A special underwater camera was lowered. It showed two oak chests and a human hand . . . Is there a treasure chamber right at the base of the Money Pit?

Nearly 200 years since its discovery, all that has been recovered from the Money Pit are three small links from a gold chain. Many theories have been suggested about who buried the treasure, but Oak Island still keeps hold of its mystery. Local people say that when the last oak tree on it dies, it will reveal its secret. Two still remain.

Vanished without trace!

It is 4 March 1918. The First World War still rages on land and at sea. In the waters of the western North Atlantic, a 19,000-tonne supply vessel, called the USS *Cyclops*, leaves Barbados and sets sail for the American port of Norfolk, Virginia.

In command of the *Cyclops* is German-born Captain Worley, a man well known for his strange behaviour. On leaving Barbados, he inexplicably orders the ship to turn suddenly to the south, away from the planned route.

Then, without warning, all contact with the *Cyclops* is lost. An air and sea search finds no trace of the *Cyclops*, nor is there sign of any wreckage. It seems that no German submarines or mines were in the area at the time of the ship's disappearance.

What happened to the *Cyclops*? Was it struck by a freak wave or blown up by bombs planted by German spies? Was it betrayed by its odd captain? An official US Navy investigation rejects these explanations, calling the incident 'one of the most baffling mysteries in the history of the Navy.'

One fascinating theory remains: that the *Cyclops* became yet another victim of the mysterious region through which it travelled . . . the so-called Bermuda Triangle.

31

The ships' graveyard

The area in which the USS *Cyclops* disappeared has been called the 'sea of lost ships' or 'the ships' graveyard'. Its actual name is the Sargasso Sea and it lies in the western region of the North Atlantic. Its most striking feature is the masses of seaweed which float on its surface. Sailors' legends tell of how ships became held forever in this web of weeds or were sucked beneath the surface in its deathly grip. Whatever the truth of these tales, there have been a series of baffling losses of ships in this region since records were started in 1800.

At the beginning of the nineteenth century, no less than three ships were mysteriously lost in this region in the space of 25 years. On 20 August 1800, the USS *Pickering* and her crew of 90 disappeared while heading for Guadeloupe, a group of islands in the Caribbean. Fourteen years later, the

Crewmen from the Ellen Austen *set out to investigate a schooner which was found abandoned near the Azores in 1881.*

The 'Philadelphia Experiment'

Could an experiment, said to have been carried out in 1943, provide a clue to the secret of the Bermuda Triangle? It was designed to test the effects of a strong magnetic field on a manned ship. The results were amazing. At first, a hazy green light surrounded the vessel. Then, both ship and crew began to disappear! Soon, all trace of them had gone! Only after the magnetic field was switched off did they become visible again! It is even said that, for some months afterwards, members of the crew were prone to vanish and then re-appear! Are magnetic forces the key to the Triangle's mystery?

USS *Wasp* vanished without trace with 140 men lost. Then, in 1824, the USS *Wildcat* and her crew of 14 went missing shortly after setting sail from Cuba.

Ships have also been found adrift, abandoned by their crew for no apparent reason. In 1881, the *Ellen Austen* was passing west of the Azores when her crew came across an abandoned schooner. Three men were placed aboard the

In 1945, five planes, like these, mysteriously vanished over what was later to be called the 'Bermuda Triangle'.

schooner, but soon afterwards a storm blew up and she became separated from the *Ellen Austen*. When she was sighted two days later, the three crewmen had also disappeared! A second crew of three went aboard the schooner. Once again, a sudden storm separated the two ships. This time, however, they were never to meet again. The schooner and her crew had vanished, leaving behind a mystery which remains unsolved to this day.

It was in 1945, after five planes vanished while on a routine training flight, that this strange region began to attract worldwide interest. Shortly before contact with the planes was lost, the pilots reported that their instruments were 'going crazy', that they had lost their bearings and that they were 'entering white water'. Because their flight path had followed a triangular route, whose apex was in direct line with the island of Bermuda, the region became known as the 'Bermuda Triangle'.

Even with the aid of modern technology, no one can explain the strange power of the Bermuda Triangle to swallow up ships and aircraft. But what is it like to experience this frightening and unknown force? Captain Don Henry was in charge of a tug which was towing an empty barge to Fort Lauderdale, USA, in 1966. The sea was calm and weather conditions were good. Without warning, the tug's compass began to spin wildly. Then, in Henry's words, 'the horizon disappeared — the water, sky and horizon all blended together. We couldn't see where we were'. The barge was covered in a milky-coloured cloud, while the sea around it became choppy and disturbed. At that moment, the tug's electrical power failed. It was slowly being pulled back into the cloud. Henry pushed the tug's throttle full ahead and, after a long struggle, managed to pull the barge clear. Later, he said that it had felt like 'being pulled in two directions at the same time'.

What theories have been offered to explain the mystery of the Bermuda Triangle? It has been suggested that violent underwater currents may suck ships to their doom in seconds or cause huge tidal waves to overwhelm them. Some have even claimed it is UFOs which hijack the ships and kidnap their crews in order to examine them? Do the remains of an ancient civilization which had advanced powers lie within the Triangle? Does it still send out pulses of

Other mysterious disappearances

1880 HMS *Atlanta* and her crew of 290 cadets disappear without trace.
1902 A German ship, the *Freya*, is discovered adrift with no crew on board. They are never found.
1932 The *John and Mary* is found abandoned in perfect weather conditions only 80 km from Bermuda.
1963 A huge freighter, the *Marine Sulphur Queen*, disappears.
1973 The *Anita*, a 20,000-tonne freighter, is lost together with her crew of 32.

In 1966, Captain Don Henry's tug, Good News, *was almost sucked into a mysterious milky-coloured cloud while sailing through the Bermuda Triangle.*

energy which cause havoc to the surrounding seas and skies? Or is the true explanation that the area is subject to strange magnetic forces which can cause planes and boats to vanish and be whisked to another time and place?

Perhaps these ideas are merely the product of people's imaginations, and there is a simple, more logical explanation to these disappearances which has been overlooked or ignored.

King Arthur's body found?

It is a cold winter's day in AD 1189. A howling wind blows across the flat lands of south-western England. In the cemetery of Glastonbury Abbey, two men are digging a large hole, watched over by a third. Huddled in his cloak, he has come from the court of King Henry II to find out if there is any truth in the stories circulating the land about a mysterious King Arthur who once ruled Britain. People have been saying that he will soon return from his final resting place on Avalon island to reclaim his kingdom.

After digging down for 2 m, the two men pause for a few minutes, sheltered from the icy blast above their heads. It is tough work in this hard earth and they want to give up, but they are told to keep going. Cursing under their breath, they begin digging again. Almost immediately their spades clang against a slab of stone. After scooping the earth away, they find a long piece of stone with a metal cross in it. Written in Latin on the cross are the words: *Here Lies Buried the Renowned King Arthur in the Isle of Avalon*. Encouraged by the man above them, the diggers continue for a further 3 m until they come across a huge coffin made out of the trunk of an oak tree. Inside it is the skeleton of a tall man.

The courtier hurries away to tell the king what he has discovered.

37

The search for Camelot

The site of King Arthur's tomb in the grounds of Glastonbury Abbey.

Below *The 'real' Camelot probably looked like this. It was not as impressive as the descriptions of it in the stories about Arthur.*

Very little is known about Britain during the Dark Ages, between AD 400 and 700. However, during Henry II's reign (from 1154 to 1189), people began to talk about a powerful Celtic people who seemed to rule much of the country during that time. Welsh and Cornish people, especially, spoke of the adventures of the Celts' king, called Arthur, and his Knights of the Round Table.

According to them, Arthur ruled from a castle with the name of Camelot, but he spent much of his time travelling around Britain in the company of his knights. They performed many brave deeds along the way, helped by a magician called Merlin. Eventually, Arthur was betrayed to his enemies by his nephew, Mordred, and fatally wounded. His faithful knights carried him to Avalon, a mysterious island somewhere in Britain, where he later died.

After they had been uncovered in 1189, Arthur's remains were stored in a chest inside the abbey. Unfortunately, this was destroyed in the sixteenth

King Arthur talks to his knights, who are sitting round the 'Round Table' of the legends. Behind Arthur is his friend and adviser, Merlin the magician.

century, along with much of the abbey, so we cannot be sure what was found in the oak coffin. But was Glastonbury Abbey the 'Avalon' of the stories? One of the reasons Henry II chose to search for Arthur at Glastonbury was because the abbey was surrounded by soggy marshes, which made it look as though it had been built on an island. Modern-day scientists have proved that there was a lot of water around the abbey in the Dark Ages, so it could well have looked like an island. Scientists have also shown that a grave in the abbey's cemetery was dug up during Henry II's reign. Whose was it? We will never know.

In many of the pictures that illustrate the stories about Arthur's life, Camelot is shown as a fairy tale castle, similar to the one in this picture.

The ghostly king

All sorts of tales are told about King Arthur. The people who live near Cadbury Hill, where Arthur probably built Camelot, will tell you about the sound of horses' hooves every Christmas Eve as he rides down to drink at the spring beside the church at the foot of the hill. Somewhere on the hill, it is also said, there is a cave with a golden gate at its entrance. If you come at the right time, the gate will be open and you can see Arthur asleep inside.

According to legend, Arthur was born in the south west of Britain, most probably in Tintagel Castle, perched on the edge of a cliff on the coast of Cornwall. Many people did not believe this because the castle was built in the Middle Ages, long after Arthur's death. However, in the 1930s, archaeologists discovered that there had been a building on the cliff before the castle and that it had probably been a Celtic monastery. So, perhaps the tales of the strange magic conjured up by Merlin which led to Arthur's birth are true, after all?

The remains of Glastonbury Abbey in Somerset, where King Arthur was buried.

Tintagel Castle, on the north coast of Cornwall, in Britain. Beneath these walls are the remains of a Celtic monastery, where Arthur was probably born.

We think we know where Arthur was born and buried, but where was Camelot, his castle? Once again, the stories pointed to somewhere in south-western Britain, to Cadbury Hill in the county of Somerset. In the summer of 1966, archaeologists made excavations there in the hope of unearthing evidence of the castle. During their work, they came across several clues suggesting that a person of great importance had lived in the fort on top of the hill at the time when Arthur is supposed to have ruled. Bits of pottery matching those found at Tintagel were found, along with the outline of a church in the shape of the Celtic cross and unlike anything built by the Romans, who came to Britain before the Celts, or the Saxons, who arrived after them.

Bit by bit, the places and events mentioned in the stories about King Arthur are being discussed by scientists, historians and archaeologists. After being passed from one generation to the next, many of the stories have become so mixed up that it is very difficult to find out which parts are true and which are false. Even so, it is still worth investigating them to try to find out what life was really like hundreds of years ago.

Archaeologists at work near Glastonbury Abbey, hoping to find material connected with King Arthur.

Did author foretell sinking of the *Titanic*?

It is the evening of 14 April 1912. The luxurious liner *Titanic* is slowly settling in the water. Her hull has been ripped open by an iceberg. Men and women are struggling to escape from the doomed ship, but there are not enough lifeboats to hold all of them. Hundreds of people know that they are going to die unless help arrives quickly.

Lifeboats, crowded with women and children, push out from the *Titanic*. Wives part from husbands for the last time. On the decks the dance band continues to play popular tunes as the water slowly rises. No help arrives before the ship sinks and 1,513 people die.

In one of the lifeboats sits a woman who cannot believe what has happened. She only recently read a novel by Morgan Robertson in which a ship named *Titan* sinks after striking an iceberg. In the book the fictional ship is the same size and carries the same number of passengers as the *Titanic*. The ship also sinks in exactly the same area of the Atlantic Ocean as the *Titanic*. How could Robertson have produced such an accurate description of the disaster before it occurred?

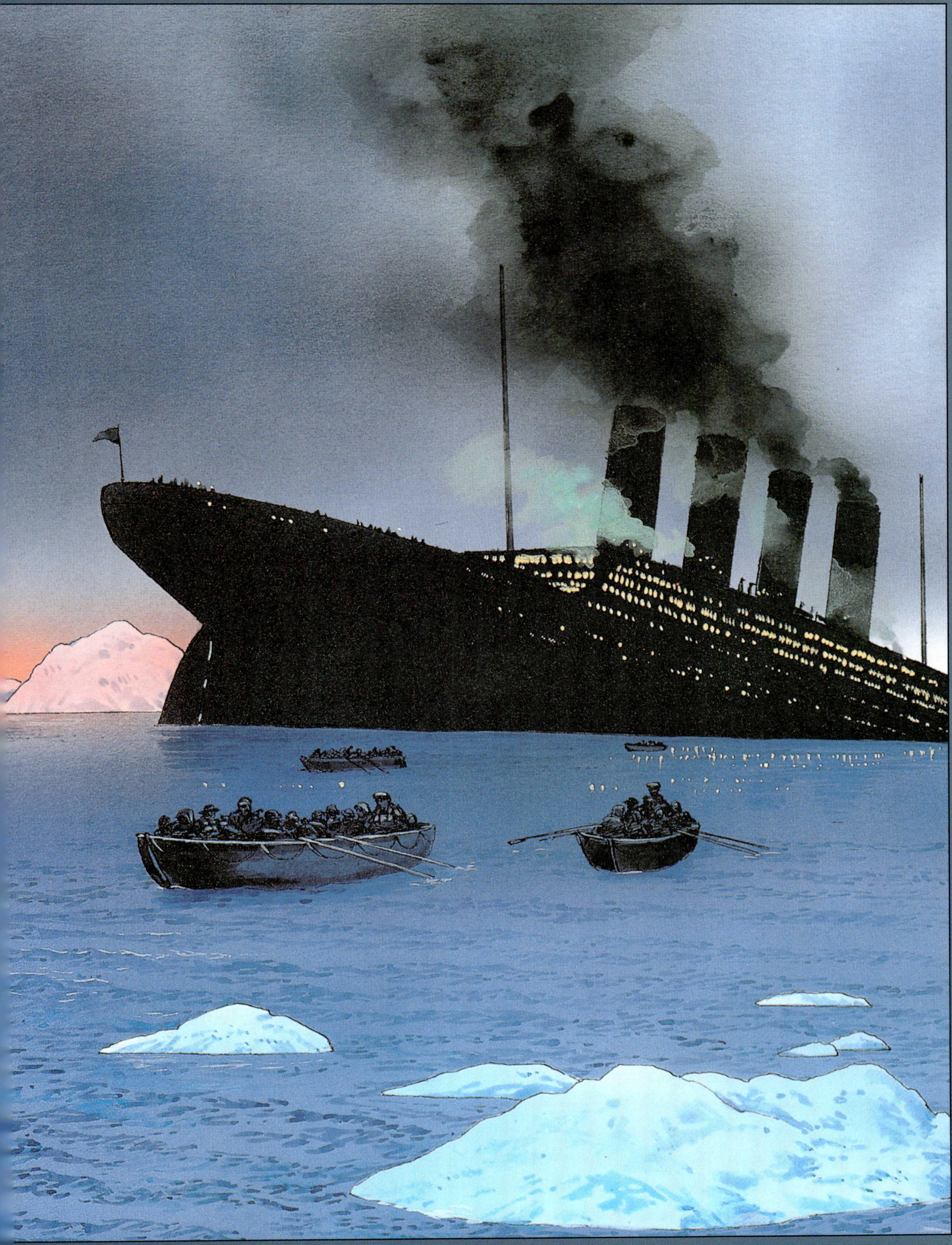

Glimpsing the future

The similarities between the imaginary *Titan* and the real-life *Titanic* seem truly extraordinary. However, sceptics point out that it could be nothing more than coincidence. The author, Morgan Robertson, might have used the idea without realizing that he was predicting the disaster. Other predictions cannot be dismissed so easily. They foretell incidents which seem highly unlikely.

On 3 May 1812, a British man dreamt that he saw the prime minister, Spencer Perceval, murdered in the lobby of the House of Commons in London. Perceval was dressed in blue and his attacker in brown. Eight days later, Spencer Perceval was shot by a man wearing a brown coat, while he himself was dressed in blue.

A more recent example of premonition happened in April 1974 when a visitor to the Tower of London heard the screams of young children. A few weeks later a terrorist bomb wounded more than a dozen children at the same spot.

The main difficulty in investigating premonitions is that they are often not recognized as such until after the event they predict. John Dunne, for instance, dreamt about a train being derailed at a certain spot in Scotland. It was only after a train accident at that spot that Dunne realized he had experienced a premonition.

Under such circumstances, it is almost impossible for researchers to be certain whether or not they are dealing with a true premonition. The witness might simply have linked a dream with a

The prophet who was wrong

In 1925 an Indian holy man, called Krishnamurti, convinced his followers that the Second Coming of Christ would occur in Sydney, Australia. He persuaded them to build a 2,000 seat stand so that they could watch the great event in comfort. After four years nothing had happened, so the stand was demolished.

similar event when there was nothing but coincidence to link the two. Other people might claim to have premonitions simply to become famous.

An important investigation into premonitions revealed these problems. On 21 October 1966 a huge coal-tip collapsed on to the Welsh village of Aberfan, killing 140 persons. Many people claimed that they had foreseen the tragedy. Dr John Barker, a psychiatrist, decided to investigate.

Barker questioned seventy-six of them. Some of their predictions were rather vague. One person dreamt that the village school had vanished, and it was, indeed, destroyed by the tip. A few days before the event, one person killed in the disaster had told her mother that her death was approaching. Though it could not be proved that any of the premonitions had occurred before the disaster, Barker noticed some interesting points. None of the premonitions had predicted the entire tragedy, only parts of it. Also, the premonitions began about three

In 1812, a British man's dream about the prime minister being assassinated turned out to be true – or was it pure coincidence?

weeks in advance and were most common the day before the disaster. Such a pattern occurs in other studies of premonitions.

Some people seem able to predict the future almost at will. The best known of them is Nostradamus, a Frenchman born in 1503. In the course of his life Nostradamus made several remarkable predictions. He once stopped an unimportant monk and told him that he would be made pope. Many years later the monk actually did become pope.

In later life, Nostradamus collected his predictions together in a series of books. Some were predictions he claimed had already come true;

The scene at the Welsh town of Aberfan on 21 October 1966 after a coal-tip had slid down on to it, killing 140 adults and children. Many people in Aberfan claimed to have foreseen the disaster.

The lucky student

On 8 March 1946 John Godley, a student at Oxford University, had a strange dream, in which he saw the names of two racehorses. On waking, Godley found that they were running in races that day. He promptly bet on them, and both won. Over the following twelve years, Godley had many similar dreams and won a lot of money.

Oxford University student John Godley won a lot of money in the 1940s after seeing the winners of horse races in his dreams.

others concerned the future. These writings were in verse, and often used complicated imagery. They are, therefore, difficult to understand accurately. For instance, one verse reads: 'Near the harbour and in two cities will be two scourges the like of which have never been seen'. Some people believe this predicts the atomic bombs dropped on the Japanese cities of Hiroshima and Nagasaki, both large ports, in 1945. Others point out that the 'prediction' is so vague that it could mean almost anything.

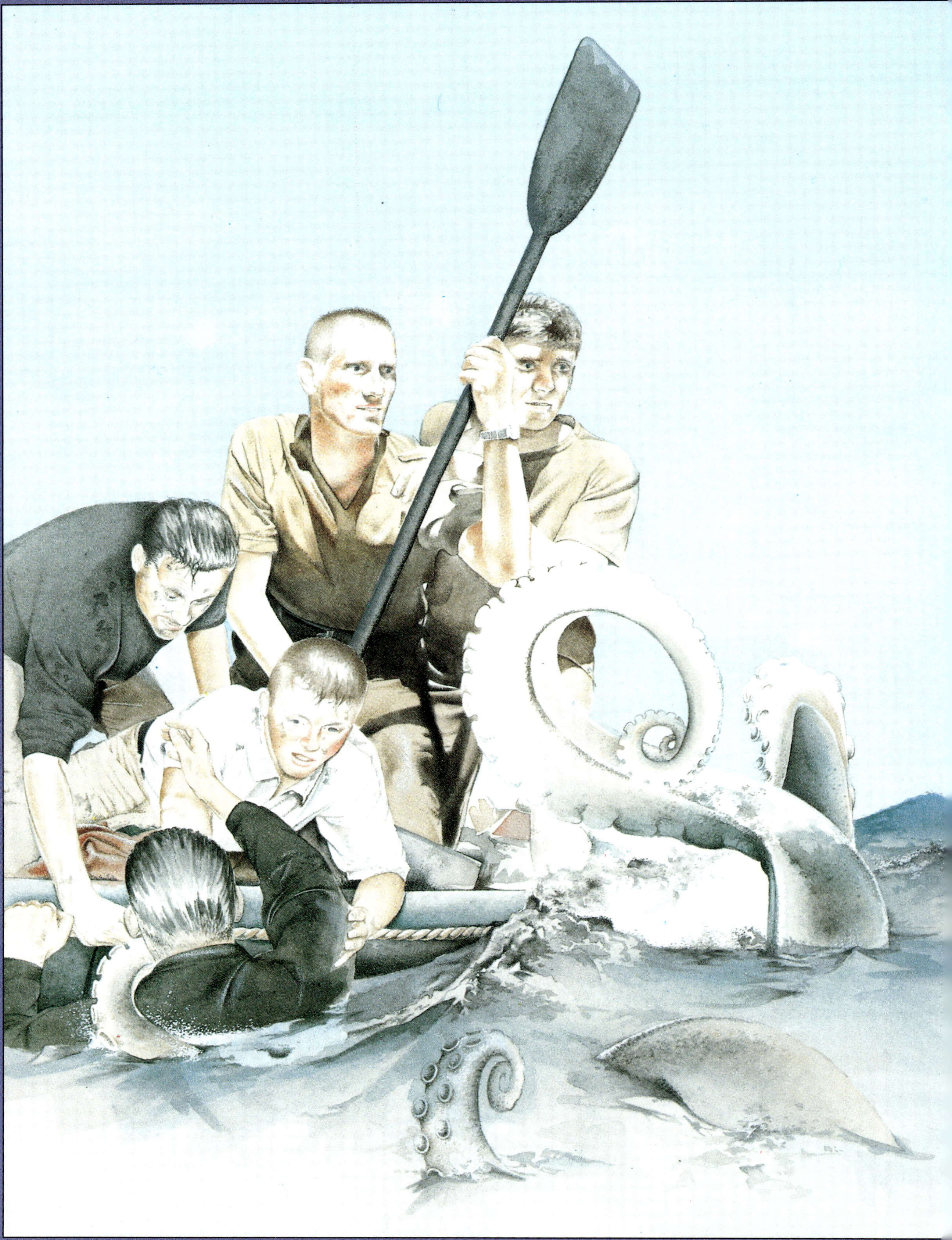

A sea monster's deathly grip

The year is 1942. Lieutenant Cox's thirst grows worse under the fierce sun. For three days, he and 11 other British sailors have been adrift in a flimsy liferaft in the remote and dangerous waters of the South Atlantic.

With horror, Cox sees a threatening dark shape in the water alongside the raft. It is at least 8 metres in length and has a broad head.

'Am I imagining things?' Cox wonders as he makes out two large eyes staring at him from beneath the waves.

Then, slowly and deliberately, a number of enormous tentacles emerge from the water. They reach out and coil around a man at the rear of the raft. Cox and the other men struggle to prise him free from the vice-like grip of the tentacles. But all their efforts are in vain. The poor victim is lifted from the raft like a baby from a cradle. He disappears, wrapped in the monster's arms.

Cox and his men, wounded in the life and death struggle, prepare for another attack. The creature clearly has the power to crush the liferaft and devour all on board. But, incredibly, it does not return. Cox, along with only two other naval officers who survive, will live to tell this frightening tale.

What kind of creature was it that attacked the liferaft on that fateful day in 1942?

Monsters of the deep

From the earliest times there have been stories and legends of strange and frightening sea monsters capable of bringing death and destruction to those who dared to venture into certain remote and unmapped areas of the oceans. Norse legend named one of these creatures the 'Kraken', a type of squid or octopus so huge that it could overturn fishing boats, whaling vessels and even ships. This frightening creature had thick, long tentacles with huge sucker pads and rows of claws to grip its prey, while its 'mouth' was a beak which was capable of cutting through wire and of piercing the side of a ship.

Could it have been a Kraken which attacked a fishing boat off Newfoundland in 1873? The two fishermen on board had prodded what appeared to be a large mass of seaweed heading for their boat and were horrified when it reared up

A painting of a huge, octopus-like Kraken attacking a merchant ship in the late eighteenth century.

Another monster of the deep is the giant sea serpent. One is said to have been spotted by the crew of HMS Daedalus *while they were rounding the Cape of Good Hope in 1848.*

in the water and seized their vessel in two huge tentacles. It looked like a large squid or octopus. Repeated blows with an axe eventually forced the wounded monster to release its deadly hold on the boat, leaving behind a piece of tentacle 6 metres long. Experts calculated that it belonged to a creature 20 metres in length.

John Starkey reports a chilling encounter with a Kraken-like creature that came alongside his naval patrol-ship in the Indian Ocean one evening in 1942. He recalls 'two cold green eyes' staring up from the water, tentacles half a metre thick and describes the creature as being longer than the ship — at least 50 metres in length! Fortunately, the monster made no attack.

Other ships have not been so lucky. In 1872, the crew of the steamer *Strathowen* claimed they saw 'a giant squid' topple a 150-tonne schooner, the *Pearl*, and drag it beneath the waves. In the 1930s, a 15,000-tonne tanker called the *Brunswick* claimed to have survived three attacks by Kraken-like monsters.

There have been many reported sightings of another legendary monster of the deep, the sea serpent. The most famous of these occurred in 1848, when sailors aboard HMS *Daedalus*, a 19-tonne frigate, spotted a strange creature while rounding the Cape of Good Hope. Captain Peter McQuhae later confirmed that it was a sea serpent, 20 metres in length, which swam alongside the *Daedalus* for over 20 minutes. The body was dark brown. Its head was raised about a metre out of the water, revealing jaws large enough to hold a fully-grown man and lined with fierce jagged teeth.

In 1852, the whaling ships the *Monongahela* and the *Rebecca Sims* were scouring the Pacific when a whale was sighted. Three longboats were lowered from the *Monongahela* in pursuit of the creature, which proved to be huge — some 45 metres in length. Stuck with harpoons, the creature's wild threshing smashed two longboats, but after a fierce struggle, it was hauled alongside the ship. Too long to take on board, only the remarkable head with its cruel teeth was cut off and preserved in a pickling vat. The *Monongahela* never reached home. Ship and crew disappeared. Wreckage was found off the coast of Alaska some weeks later. There was no explanation. Was the ship

Opposite *This map shows where sea monsters, of all shapes and sizes, have supposedly been sighted over the years.*

A sea serpent, with a head like a turtle's, was said to have attacked a liferaft in 1962 and carried off four of its occupants.

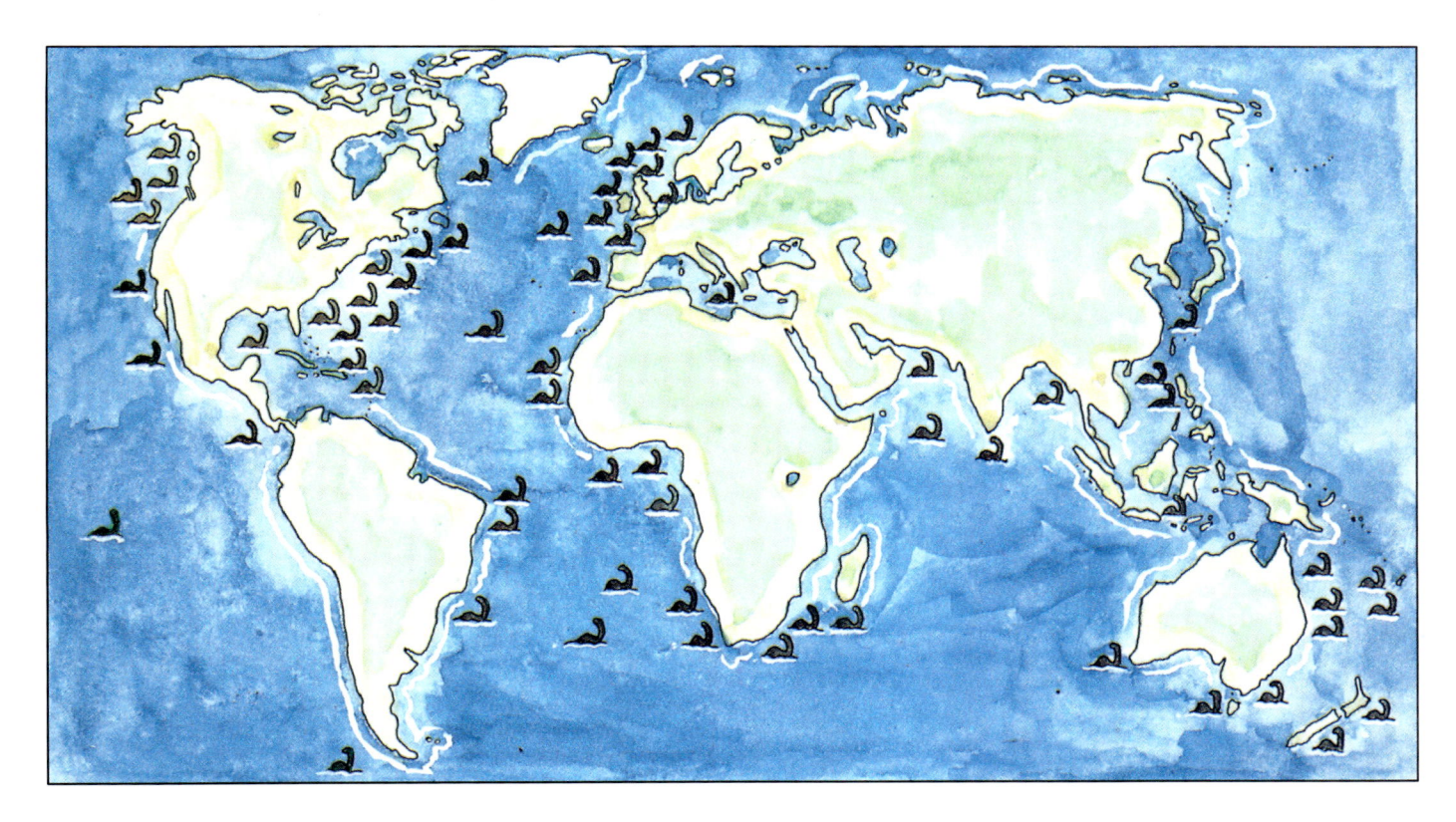

Below *A photograph of 'Morgawr', a monster reportedly seen off the coast of Cornwall, south-western Britain, in February 1976. It was about 8 metres long.*

attacked and destroyed by another monster?

In 1962, a liferaft carrying five men was attacked by a sea serpent. Its head and neck resembled that of a turtle and stretched over 4 metres out of the water. Hissing horribly, it gave off a foul-smelling odour of rotting fish. After capsizing the raft, the monster carried off four of the men, leaving one survivor to recount the terrifying tale.

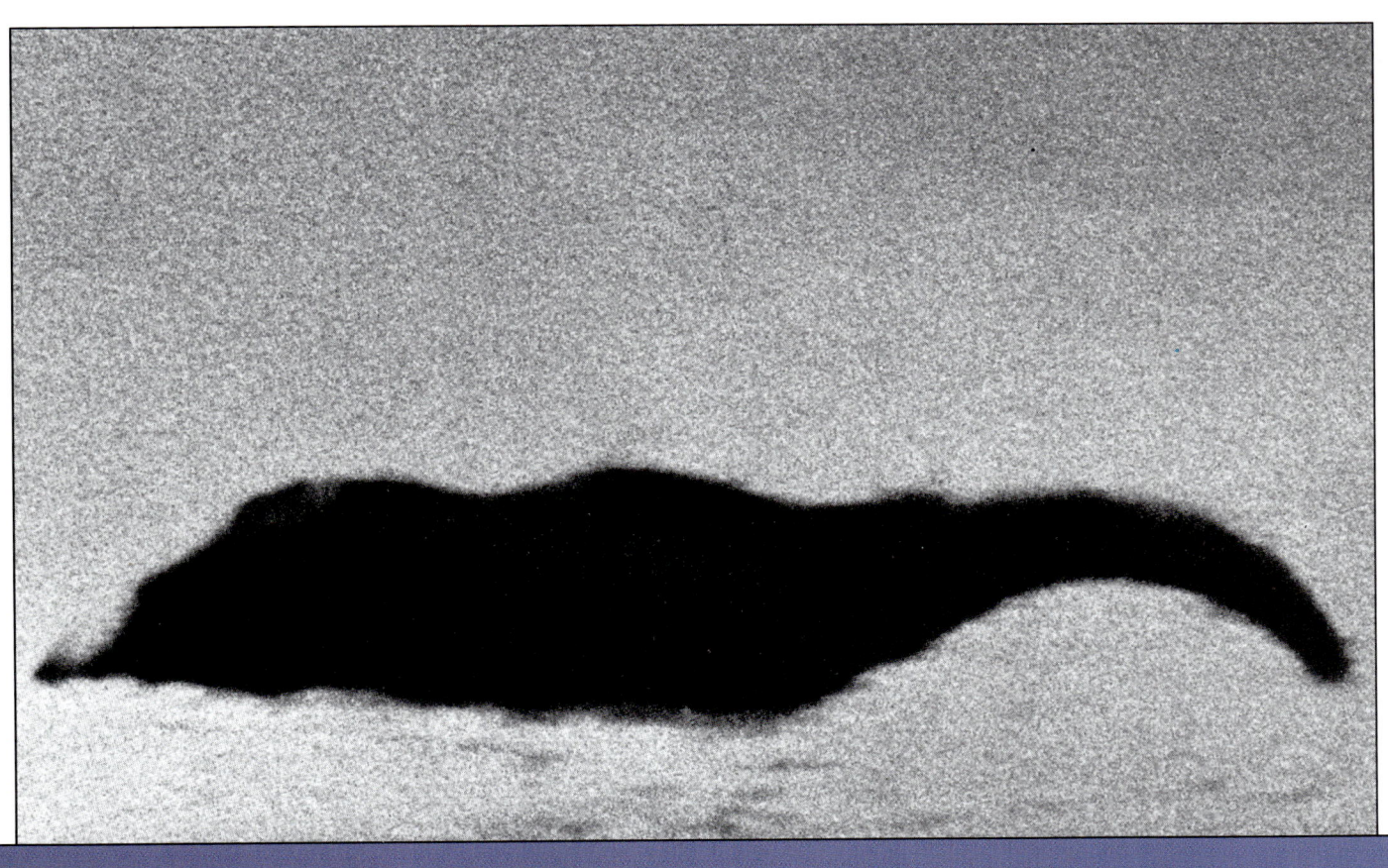

The *Architeuthis*

In 1857, the Kraken was given a Latin name by scientists, *Architeuthis*. The largest specimen ever measured was washed up on St. Augustine's Beach, Florida, in 1896. Its tentacles measured about 9 metres and its original length was estimated to have been 20 metres. Many sailors claim to have seen giant *Architeuthis* doing battle with sperm whales. One captured sperm whale had sucker scars measuring 36 cm on its body, suggesting that its foe measured around 150 metres – half the height of the Eiffel Tower in Paris!

Above A sea serpent which, it is said, was seen frequently off the coast of Massachusetts, USA, in the 1800s.

Right A nineteenth-century picture making fun of people who said they had seen monsters at sea.

A sea monster photographed in Stonehaven Bay, Hook Island, Australia, on 12 December 1964.

Some sea monsters choose to haunt waters closer to land. One such creature is supposed to roam the Strait of Georgia, between Vancouver Island and British Columbia, off the west coast of Canada. It was first sighted by native North Americans long before white settlers arrived, and is known as Cadborosaurus or 'Caddy'. In this century it has been seen by over 100 people and has been described as being a sea serpent 15 metres long, with huge, wide jaws.

In 1965, a Belgian zoologist, Dr Bernard Heuvelmans, began the most detailed study of sea serpents to date. He examined 587 sightings dating from 1639 to 1964 and concluded that 358 were genuine. From these, he divided the sea serpents into nine types. Could the oceans really be roamed by so many species of sea monster? If so, how many more are yet to be discovered?

Monsters sighted around the world

1882 Llandudno, North Wales: 'a large, dark, undulating creature as big as a large steamer.'

1893 Cape Town, South Africa: 'a giant eel, 25 metres long, with jaws 2 metres wide.'

1964 Great Barrier Reef, Australia: 'a gigantic beast, 20 metres long, with jaws 1 metre wide.'

1966 North Atlantic: 'a writhing, twisting monster, between 10 and 12 metres long.'

1976 Cornwall, England: a monster, nicknamed 'Morgawr' (sea giant), measuring about 8 metres, is spotted and photographed.

The Mantell mystery

It is 7 January 1948. In the skies above Kentucky, in the USA, four F-51 fighter aircraft led by Captain Thomas Mantell are nearing the end of a routine training flight from Georgia.

On the ground below, Fort Knox military police report the sighting of an unusual object flying at great speed through the air. At a nearby airfield, the object is picked up on radar screens and then seen through binoculars by an amazed observer:

> 'It's very white and looks like an umbrella!' he cries, 'I just don't know what it is! It appears to have a red border at the bottom at times . . . and a red border at the top at times!'

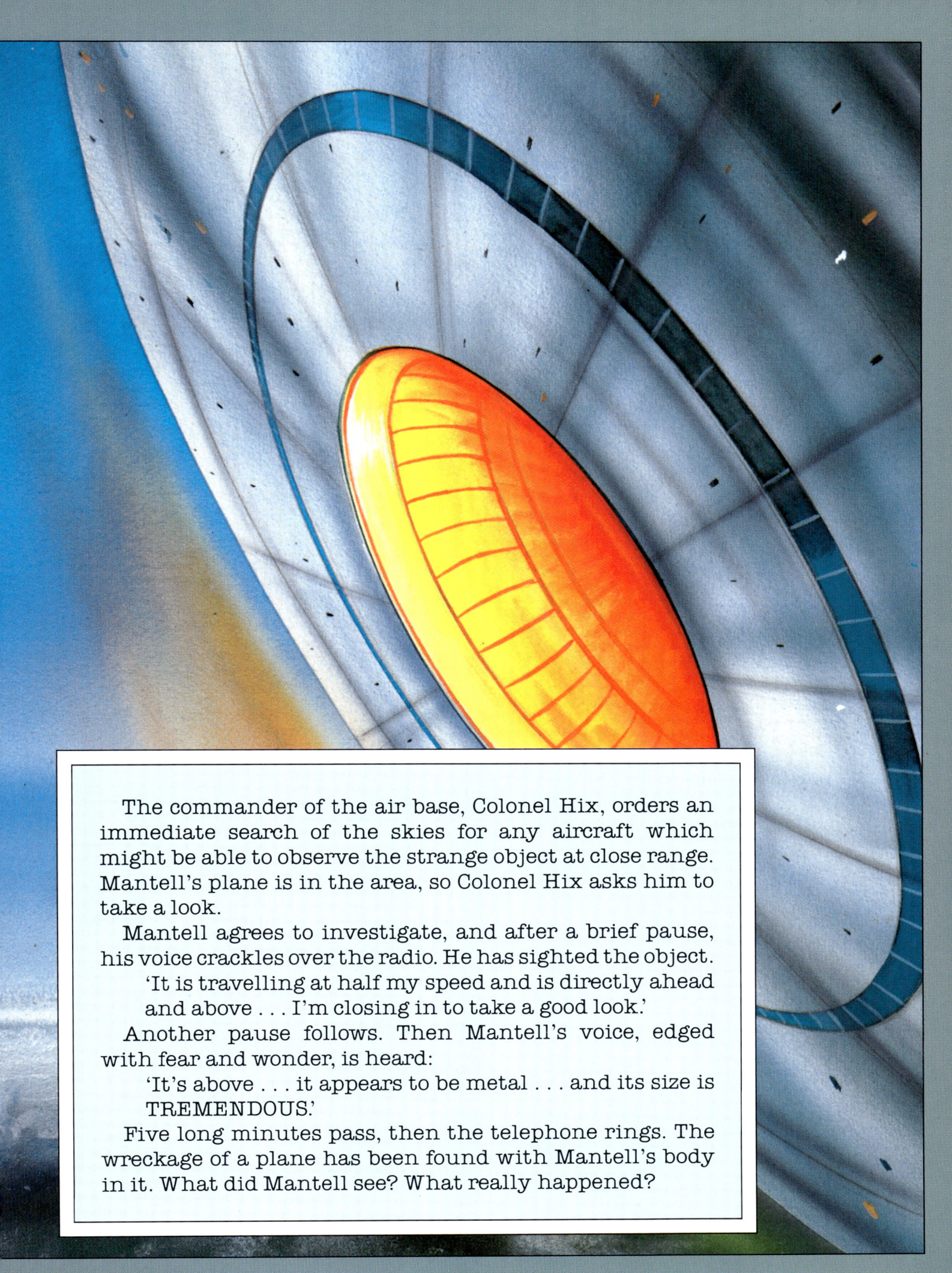

The commander of the air base, Colonel Hix, orders an immediate search of the skies for any aircraft which might be able to observe the strange object at close range. Mantell's plane is in the area, so Colonel Hix asks him to take a look.

Mantell agrees to investigate, and after a brief pause, his voice crackles over the radio. He has sighted the object.

'It is travelling at half my speed and is directly ahead and above . . . I'm closing in to take a good look.'

Another pause follows. Then Mantell's voice, edged with fear and wonder, is heard:

'It's above . . . it appears to be metal . . . and its size is TREMENDOUS.'

Five long minutes pass, then the telephone rings. The wreckage of a plane has been found with Mantell's body in it. What did Mantell see? What really happened?

Out of this world?

Since 1947, over 100,000 people have reported some kind of UFO experience. On average about 40 new cases are reported each day around the world. Witnesses have varied in age, sex, background and beliefs. In 30 countries there are now permanent observers who keep a constant watch on the sky for UFO appearances.

Nowadays, sightings come in 'waves'; that is, an unusually high number of UFO reports in a particular region or country over a short period of time. In one particular 'wave' in the USA in 1973, there were over 920 UFO sightings within the space of a few weeks.

Interest in UFOs has increased largely because we now have more knowledge about space and the nature of the universe. The facts seem to support more strongly the idea that there are forms of intelligent life other than ourselves.

A view towards the centre of the Milky Way. In the universe there are many galaxies, and millions of stars and planets. It is very possible that some of these worlds may be inhabited by other forms of life.

Our own galaxy (the Milky Way) is made up of over 100,000 million stars that are similar to our sun. As in our solar system, each of these stars is surrounded by a number of planets. Can it be that our solar system is the only one of these to support life?

Over the past thirty years, we have begun to explore space ourselves, using both manned spacecraft and unmanned probes. We have begun to unfold some of the secrets of our closest planets and stars. Each discovery adds more to our sense of wonder at galaxies other than our own.

The Pioneer 10 spacecraft in orbit around Jupiter. As we gather more and more information about the planets in our solar system, it seems certain that there is little chance of life existing on any of them.

Are UFOs a fascinating glimpse of other worlds, of minds and machines more advanced than ours? What are UFOs like? They are often described as seeming like balls of light which change shape and colour again and again. Sometimes they are shaped like stars and crosses, or even like an egg. The most frequently-described sightings are cigar-shaped UFOs and flying discs that look like saucers.

All reports agree that UFOs can travel at great speed. If these craft actually do come from outer space, they would certainly have to be able to travel huge distances in a short period of time. For example, to reach earth's nearest star, Alpha Centauri, would take 4.5 years even travelling at the speed of light (300,000 kilometres per second).

How might UFOs travel? One theory is that UFOs create an artificial field of gravity in front of them which they fall into. This gravity field would also explain why some UFOs appear to have had strange effects on machines here on earth. Another explanation is that UFOs are able to de-materialize, beam their atoms across space and time, and re-materialize at their journey's end. Some scientists believe that UFOs are nuclear powered and are pushed through space by a stream of radiation.

Humankind has achieved a great deal in space exploration in a short time. However, even with advanced spacecraft, which could travel at the speed of light, such as the one in the picture above, it would still take 4.5 years to reach the nearest star.

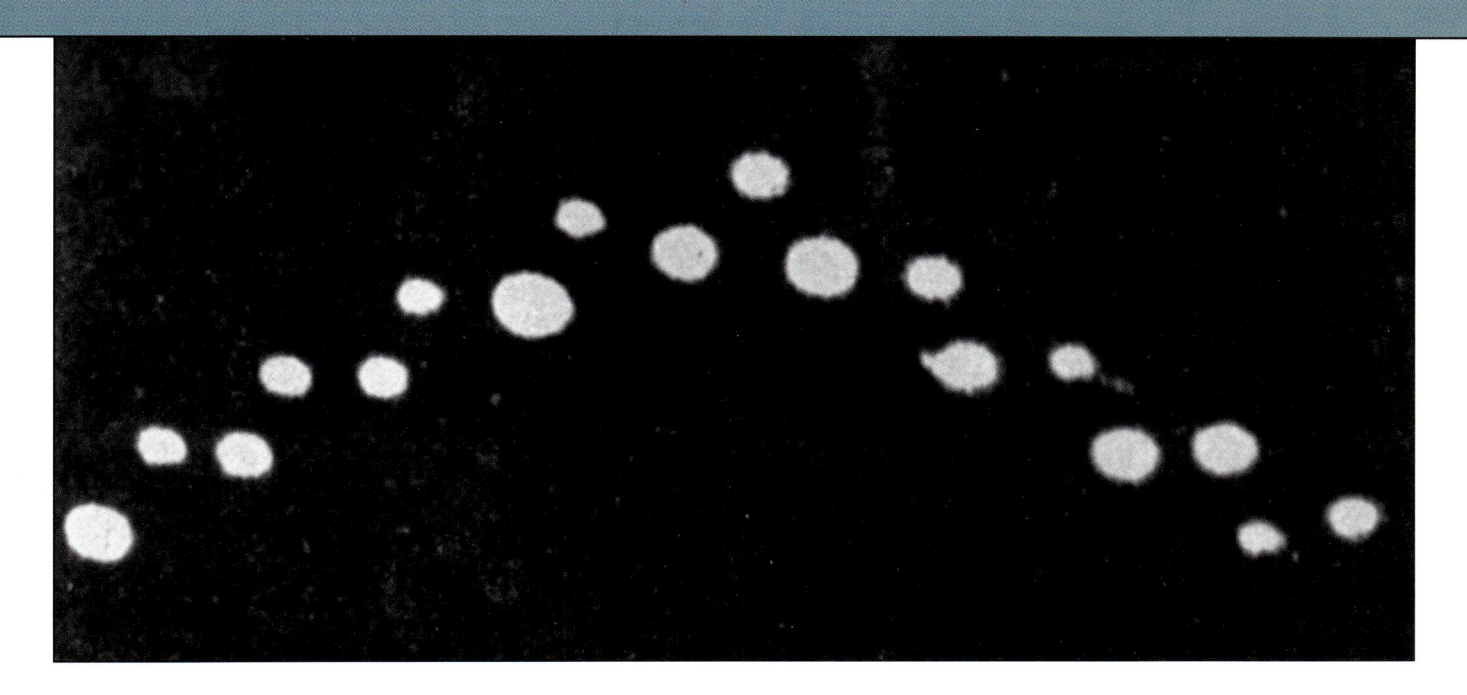

Explanations of where UFOs come from range from remote areas of the earth itself, like the North Pole, to other planets in our solar system. The first explanation is highly unlikely, and the other planets in our solar system are thought to be either too hot or too cold to support life forms. Could UFOs come from beyond the solar system? One amazing suggestion is that there are a number of universes that are existing at the same time, parallel to one another. Are UFOs visitors from these parallel worlds?

A formation of lights, possibly UFOs, seen over Texas, USA, on 30 August 1951.

The mystery of Sirius B

The Dogon tribe of Mali in West Africa have an ancient myth which claims that long ago they were visited by amphibious beings from Sirius, the brightest star in the night sky. Dogon belief states that Sirius has two invisible companions. One is a star with a nearly circular orbit; the other is a star 'heavier than all the material on earth', which orbits Sirius every 50 years.

In 1862, Sirius B, a white-dwarf star was discovered by astronomers. It is made of very dense material and takes 50 years to orbit Sirius. Without the aid of astronomical equipment, how could the Dogon know this?
Above right: a Dogon sketch of the orbit of Sirius B; note how closely this resembles the actual orbit path (**below right**).

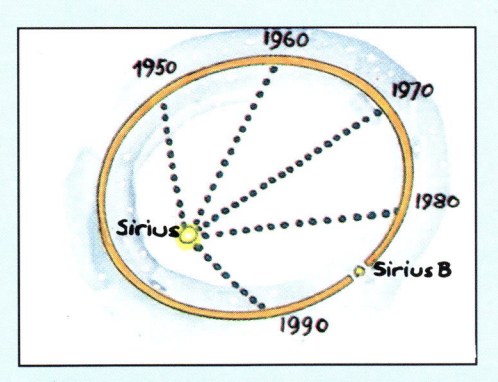

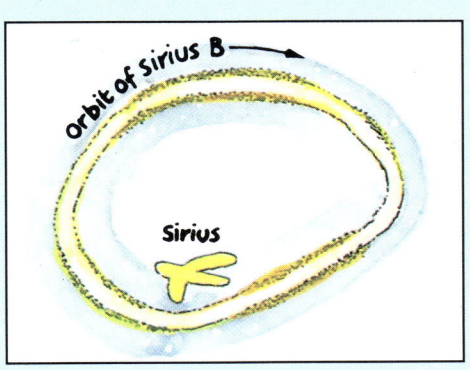

Index

Aberfan 45, 46
Alpha Centauri 60
America 21, 30, 34, 52, 54
   UFO sightings over 56
archaeologists 14
Architeuthis see Kraken
Arthur, King 36–41
Atlantic Ocean 7–9, 30, 32, 33, 49, 55
Atlantis 7–11
Australia 44, 55
Avalon 36, 38, 39
Azores 21, 33

Bacon, Francis 9
Bahamas 7, 11
Barker, Dr John 45
Bermuda Triangle 30, 33, 34
Bimini Island 7, 10
bluestones 17
Britain 10, 21, 36, 38, 40, 41, 44, 47, 49, 55
Brunswick 51

Cadborosaurus ('Caddy') 55
Cadbury Hill 40, 41

Camelot 38, 40, 41
Canada 24, 55
Cape of Good Hope 18, 51, 52
Caribbean 22, 30, 32–34
Cayce, Edgar 10
Celtic ceremony 13
Celts 14, 38, 40, 41
Central America 32
charnel houses 15, 17
Courtenay, James 21

Dark Ages 38, 39
de-materialize 60
disappearing ships 21, 30, 32–34, 52
Donnelly, Ignatius 10
dreams 45, 47
druids 14
Dunne, John 44

Ellen Austen 33, 34

First World War 30, 47
Flying Dutchman 18, 19
France 46, 47

galaxies 59
Germany 23, 30, 47
   Celts from 14
Glastonbury Abbey 36–40
Godley, John 47
gravity 60
Great Cursus 16
Greece 8

Heel Stone 15
henge 15, 16
Henry, Capt Don 34, 35
Henry II, King 36–39
Heuvelmans, Dr Bernard 55
historians 14
HMS *Daedalus* 51, 52

India 44
Indian Ocean 51
Indonesia 18, 20

Japan 47